Basic Needlepoint

Basic Needlepoint

by Maxine Searls

Published in association with *Parade Magazine*

GROSSET & DUNLAP
A National General Company
Publishers · New York

Library of Congress Catalog Card Number: 71-156324
ISBN: 0-448-02091-2

Printed in the United States of America

PARADE – P. O. Box #99
Kensington Station, Brooklyn, New York 11218

Please send me_____ copies/Diet Watchers Guide

_____ copies/Living with Arthritis

_____ copies/Macrame

_____ copies/Complete Kitchen Guide

_____ copies/Help for Your Headache

_____ copies/The Home Kebob Cookbook

_____ copies/Personality Parade

_____ copies/Babysitter Bulletin Board

I am enclosing $1. (no stamps) for each book ordered above.

NAME_____

ADDRESS_____

CITY_____ STATE_____ ZIP_____

EIGHT HELPFUL BOOKS FROM PARADE

1. THE DIET WATCHERS GUIDE: If losing weight is your number one resolution, Parade is right with you offering an invaluable book that tells how to do it.

2. LIVING WITH ARTHRITIS: Don't rely on quack cures and remedies. Know the truth about arthritis written by a well known doctor specializing in its treatment.

3. MACRAME: This book offers detailed instructions for the many new knots. It has 35 different ornamental knots that you can use to create fashionable accessories yourself.

4. COMPLETE KITCHEN GUIDE: Be your own gourmet chef. This one volume includes everything any cook needs to know about utencils, food stuffs, weight measures, cooking times, freezing, herbs and spices and much more. A must for everyone.

5. HELP FOR YOUR HEADACHE: Do you know the truth about the most universal human ailment? Don't be led astray. This book explains what causes them, when you should see a doctor and may help you relieve many tensions.

6. THE HOME KEBOB COOKBOOK: Be the talk of your neighborhood. This book enables you to prepare various types of kebobs for parties and entertaining or just for a good family dinner.

7. PERSONALITY PARADE: Now available in book form. It contains over 350 outstanding questions and answers to items you have always wondered about.

8. BABYSITTER BULLETIN BOARD: A must for a family with young children. The 8½ X 11" Board has space provided for permanent emergency information and there is a 50 sheet tear off pad attached covering special instructions on where you can be reached the time you are away from home.

To Alan and Damion

CONTENTS

INTRODUCTION 1

CHAPTER 1 MATERIALS 3

Canvas.. 3
Yarn... 5
Needles...................................... 6
Frame.. 6

CHAPTER 2 PREPARATION 7

Canvas....................................... 7
Joining Canvas............................... 8
Pattern...................................... 9
Yarn... 12
Frame.. 13

CHAPTER 3 STITCHES 14

Special Considerations....................... 14
General Working Instructions
   (*Making a Sampler*)........................ 15
Starting and Ending Off...................... 17

True Needlepoint Stitches...................... 19
   1. Continental   2. Basketweave
Cross Stitch Variations........................ 23
   *1. Half Cross   2. Cross   3. Knit   4. Slanting
   Gobelin   5. Oblong Cross   6. Three Stitch
   Cross   7. Double Cross   8. Large and Small
   Cross   9. Rice*
Diagonal Stitches............................. 32
   *1. Wide Gobelin   2. Encroaching Gobelin
   3. Knotted   4. Florentine Mosaic   5. Hungarian
   Mosaic   6. Cashmere   7. Scotch   8. Milanese
   9. Checkerboard   10. Checker   11. Byzantine
   12. Jacquard*
Tree Stitches................................. 47
   1. Stem   2. Fern   3. Herringbone   4. Leaf
Upright Stitches.............................. 53
   *1. Upright Gobelin   2. Brick   3. Parisian
   4. Hungarian   5. Old Florentine   6. Bargello*
Novelty Stitches............................. 60
   *1. Diamond Eyelet   2. Star   3. Chain   4. Loop
   and Fringe*

CHAPTER 4 FINISHING.................... 68
Cleaning...................................... 68
Blocking...................................... 68
Mitering Corners............................. 69
Mounting Pictures............................ 70
Mounting Seat Covers......................... 71
Gluing....................................... 72
Sewing....................................... 72

CHAPTER 5 PROJECTS 74
Repeat-Design Belt........................... 74
Concentric-Square Pillow..................... 78

Introduction

Needlepoint is the art of covering a canvas with stitches. While it may be used to paint with stitches, so to speak, producing fine pictures, wall hangings and other decorative items, its practical applications are virtually unlimited, and surprisingly few have been explored. Upholstery, rugs, throw pillows, door stops and pin-cushions are but a few of the more popular needlepoint items being made today. Yet this type of stitchery lends itself remarkably well to belts, chokers, headbands, handbags, stuffed toys, unusual trim for capes or skirts, and exquisite vests, boleros and ponchos. By experimenting with different canvas, yarn, stitches and color combinations, almost any effect can be achieved.

There has been a recent "revival" of needlepoint in the United States and consequently there is a veritable glut of prepared needlepoint kits to suit almost any taste. They come in 2 forms. The first has the main pattern already worked and only the background needs to be filled in. The second comes supplied either with a canvas on which the design has been painted, or with canvas and a chart; and both include sufficient yarn to complete the article in the designer's choice of colors and stitches. The first type, in my opinion, is boring and uncreative. The second is convenient, especially if the designer's taste and yours are compatible. Blank canvas and a vast assortment of yarns are available, however, and it's more creative and a great deal cheaper to work your own designs.

This book shows you, clearly and simply, all the basics of needlepoint. It will, I hope, be equally useful to both the novice and the somewhat experienced needlepointer. If you can thread a needle and count, you can do beautiful needlepoint.

CHAPTER 1
Materials

CANVAS

The fabric on which needlepoint stitches are worked is called a canvas. It consists of evenly spaced horizontal and vertical threads with square holes between.

There are 2 basic types of canvas: single-thread or mono, and double-thread or penelope (Diagram 1). Some stitches are best worked on a particular type, but most stitches can

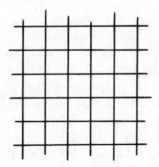 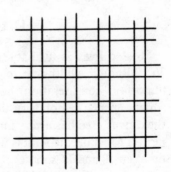

Diagram 1

3

be worked satisfactorily on either. This will be further discussed in Chapter 3. Generally, the double thread of penelope canvas is regarded as a single thread and the needle is worked only in the large holes. However, it is possible to work part of a piece with twice as many stitches per 1″ as the rest of the piece if the double thread is considered as 2 separate threads and the needle is worked into both the large and small holes (Diagram 2).

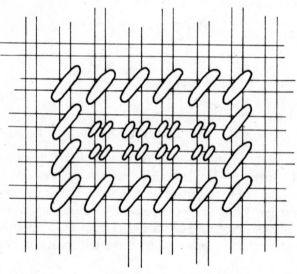

Diagram 2

Most canvas is available in widths ranging from 27″ to 36″, although widths up to 54″ may be obtained. The most important consideration, however, is the gauge (number of squares per 1″). For very fine work, known as petit point, the canvas used has a very fine gauge of as many as 20 squares per 1″. Most needlepoint is worked on canvas with a gauge of between 10 and 14 squares. Large work, known as gros point and suitable for rugs, is usually worked on a canvas with a coarse gauge of only 4 to 6 squares per 1″.

The color of the canvas is unimportant, as it is covered by the stitches. The most common colors, however, are white and ecru. Canvas is available with every fifth or tenth thread done in a contrasting color, and this is useful for aligning work and for quick counting.

Whichever type of canvas you choose, it should be stiff and have smooth, continuous threads. If it feels gummy, it is of poor quality, and it won't work or last well.

YARN

The main consideration when selecting a type of yarn is whether it will completely cover the canvas with the kind of stitch used. Other considerations are fibre content and quality. A knitting yarn generally has a shorter, more wiry fibre than that of yarn made specially for needlepoint, and it will tend to pill or ball with wear. A poor quality yarn will not cover the canvas evenly and may fray or split while being worked.

A 10 to 12 gauge canvas is best worked with crewel, tapestry or Persian yarn, the last of which is my favorite. The quality is far superior to crewel yarn and the colors are more vibrant than the tapestry yarns. It is, however, often more expensive than the others. For petit point, or fine work, silk or embroidery threads may be used instead of fingering yarn. Rug yarn is suitable for gros point, or large work.

Most yarns are composed of several strands. If your yarn is too thick for the work being done, unravel it and use only the number of strands required to cover the canvas adequately. Conversely, if your yarn is too thin, double or treble it, or use a full thread, plus however many additional strands are required. Interesting shading or color combinations may be obtained by combining strands of different color yarn.

Yarn is sold by weight or by length. To estimate the yardage, work 1 sq." using the canvas, yarn and stitch intended for the piece and multiply the amount of yarn you used by the total area to be covered. Allow extra for the beginning and end of each length of thread. Unless you know how much yardage there is to the ounce, pound or gram of yarn which is sold by weight, it is difficult to estimate how much yarn you will require. It is generally advised that you buy more than you think you will need, because it's often difficult to match dye lots, and extra yarn can always be used in another project.

NEEDLES

Always use a blunt, large-eye tapestry needle. Crewel and embroidery needles are too sharp and might split your canvas thread, or yarn. Sizes range from 15, the largest, to 26, the smallest. Select the size according to the canvas and yarn to be used. A good rule of thumb is the lower the needle size, the coarser the gauge.

It is convenient when working with several colors to have each color threaded on a separate needle. This eliminates the inconvenience of threading your needle each time you change color.

FRAMES

Needlepoint may be worked in the hand or in a frame. Small pieces may be worked on hand-held, round or oval embroidery hoops, while a larger piece would be better worked on a larger frame that clamps to a chair or table, or that has a stand. Adjustable square frames onto which the canvas has to be sewn (see Chapter 2) are also available. A piece worked in a frame requires little or no blocking, but if no frame is used the needlepoint is more flexible and portable. The choice is up to you.

CHAPTER 2
Preparation

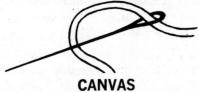

CANVAS

This section is primarily for those working their own designs. If you are working from a kit, your canvas needs little or no preparation.

If your canvas has any creases or folds, press them out with a dry iron. Never use steam. Place your canvas with the selvedge running vertically, i.e., along the side. (The selvedge is the edge where the threads are very tightly woven.)

Bear in mind that as you work, your stitches will "tighten up" your canvas. A piece of unworked canvas $12'' \times 12''$ might only measure $11\frac{1}{2}'' \times 11\frac{1}{2}''$ when worked. This tightening up will vary according to the tension of your work and the type of stitch used. If your project has to be a certain size it is advisable to allow for this tightening-up factor when you measure your unworked canvas for marking. Measure a $1''$ square (or larger) on your unworked canvas. Work it in the desired stitch. Measure the shrinkage and multiply by first the length and then the width of your finished project. Add this extra allowance when marking your pattern on the canvas.

7

Before cutting the canvas, measure according to the stitch you plan to use. If you are using a stitch covering, for example, 3 horizontal and 5 vertical meshes or squares, measure your piece so that you have a multiple of 3 meshes in the width and a multiple of 5 meshes in the length. Be sure to cut vertically and horizontally, even if you are doing a round or shaped piece, such as a vest or other article of clothing.

To make clothing, it is best to use a simple commercial pattern. When you have chosen the one you want, *test it for fit* by making it up in muslin — the last thing you want is a beautifully worked needlepoint garment that doesn't fit! The next step is to trace the pattern on the canvas, using any of the methods described below. Mark along the cutting line, making sure that the grain line of the pattern is exactly matched along a single vertical thread of the canvas. Include the dart lines, if any, keeping in mind that you will not be working the area inside.

Leave a seam allowance according to your project. A belt or pillow requires about $\frac{1}{2}''$ seam allowance, while a picture that will be framed or a seat cover needs as much as 3″. This seam allowance must be left on all sides.

The raw edges of your canvas must now be covered or they will fray and catch on your working thread. One way to do this is to whip or oversew these edges. A simpler and more efficient method is to cover them with masking tape. Cut the tape the length of the edge to be covered, place the lengthwise center of the tape along the edge and fold down on the upper and lower sides of the canvas. Repeat for all raw edges.

JOINING CANVAS

It will sometimes be necessary to join 2 or more pieces of canvas, if, for example, you are making a large wall hanging or rug. This is very simple to do.

Work to within about 1″ of the joining point. Trim the

vertical lengths of both pieces of canvas next to a vertical thread so that no horizontal threads stick out. Overlap about $\frac{1}{2}''$, and baste in place with white or beige cotton sewing thread, depending on the color canvas. This basting thread need not be removed, as your needlepoint will cover it. Do your needlepoint over the double thicknesses of canvas as if they were a single thickness.

PATTERN

If you are working from a kit, your pattern has either been painted directly on the canvas in colors approximating those of the yarn, or you have been supplied with a chart. The latter resembles graph paper, with each square representing a stitch. There is a color key, and a stitch key.

What if you want to do your own design? Even the person with little or no artistic talent can do it. The most intricate picture or design, taken from a magazine, postcard, children's coloring book or whatever, may be easily reproduced in the size you want.

If the picture is the same size as the project to be worked, trace it. If you are using a large-gauge canvas, place the tracing paper *beneath* the canvas and with a waterproof felt tip pen, draw the pattern directly on your canvas. If the design on the tracing paper is not clearly visible beneath the canvas, place the tracing paper on top of the canvas with carbon paper in between so that when the traced pattern is redrawn it will be transferred onto the canvas. Always make sure to align the horizontals and verticals of your canvas with those of your picture.

If you want to enlarge or reduce the design, draw a square or rectangle around either the original or the traced version. Mark off equidistant points ($\frac{1}{4}''$ to $1''$, depending on the intricacy of the pattern and your drawing talents) on all 4 sides. Join these points horizontally and vertically so that a grid is formed. On another piece of tracing paper or on graph paper, draw a square or rectangle the desired size of your project. (If you do not have paper large enough for the size design you want, join several smaller pieces which you put together with staples or transparent tape.) Mark off *the same number* of equidistant points as you did on the original, and join them as before. Your squares will be larger or smaller

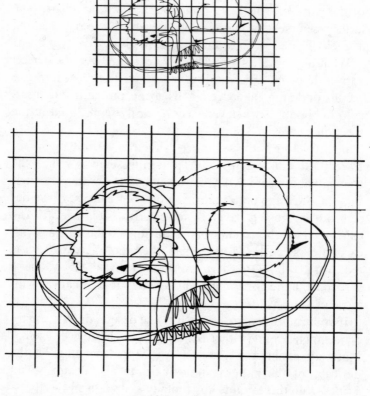

Diagrams 3a, 3b

depending on whether you are enlarging or reducing your design. Now, square by square, copy the design from the original (see Diagrams 3a, 3b). Using one of the above described methods, transfer this to your canvas, without the grids. Once more, be sure to keep your horizontals and verticals "true."

If you are working with only a few colors, you may not need any further markings on your canvas. If you want or need to color in your pattern, however, use waterproof felt tip pens, or oil paints diluted with turpentine, in colors approximating those to be worked. *Never use a water-based medium,* because even the perspiration on your hands as you work is enough to make the colors run.

If these materials are not available, you may tramé your work (Diagram 4). This is a means of marking your work with yarn and is best suited to penelope canvas. Each section is traméed in the color that will later be used for the needlepoint stitch. Only 1 strand of yarn is used and the stitches run horizontally along the double threads of the canvas.

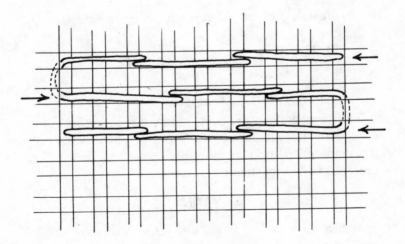

Diagram 4

Work the first and every odd row from right to left: even rows are worked left to right. Bring your needle up between the double threads in the top right-hand corner. Do a long straight stitch towards the left and bring your needle up 1 mesh to the right so that a tiny backstitch is formed. Repeat to end of row then work second row, left to right. Stagger the back stitches so that they do not fall directly below the other. If they do, a ridge will form.

Some kits come with the pattern traméed rather than painted. Tramé is useful if your thread does not fully cover the canvas; and it can also provide good padding for such items as seat covers.

If you are doing a geometric or repeat design, it might be easier to work from a chart. Using graph paper and having each square correspond to 1 needlepoint stitch, mark with symbols to designate different colors. For example:

☒ black
☑ white
☑ red
⊟ green

If you are doing several different stitches but working in only a single color:

☒ half cross
☺ knotted
☑ mosaic
⊟ gobelin

You might find it convenient, when you are working from a chart, to mark every fifth or tenth row of your canvas. Using a waterproof felt tip pen, mark horizontal and vertical lines exactly on a row of squares.

YARN

The length of your working thread should be between 18″ and 24″. The reason a longer thread is not used is that friction, caused by moving the needle in and out of the canvas, frays the yarn and weakens the stitches. The longer thread is also more tedious to work with.

FRAME

If you are using a round or oval frame, simply clamp the canvas between the pair of hoops. If you are using a square frame, the canvas has to be sewn onto the frame, as shown in Diagram 5.

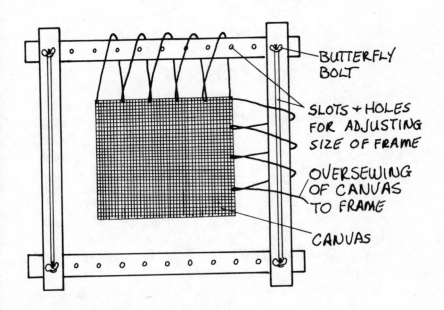

BUTTERFLY BOLT

SLOTS + HOLES FOR ADJUSTING SIZE OF FRAME

OVERSEWING OF CANVAS TO FRAME

CANVAS

Diagram 5

Remember, however, it is not necessary to use a frame. No matter how badly misshapen a piece becomes in working, it can be blocked back into shape (see Chapter 4).

CHAPTER 3
Stitches

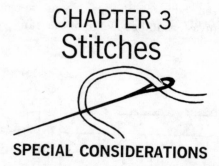

SPECIAL CONSIDERATIONS

Your canvas, as you will by now have noticed, consists of interwoven horizontal and vertical threads. The stitches used to cover these threads are either diagonal, horizontal or vertical, or a combination of these. Similarly, the rows of stitches are worked either horizontally, vertically or diagonally. Because of this, it is impossible to obtain a true curve in needlepoint — a curve will always be "stepped." This can be minimized by keeping your curves gradual, by using a large design, or by working on a fine-gauge canvas. If this is not enough, you can embroider an outline stitch over your needlepoint once it is completed.

Some stitches, generally the smaller, simpler ones, are best suited to detailed pattern work; others that cover larger areas and are quickly worked are best suited to backgrounds; while still others which have interesting textural effects in and of themselves are best suited to simple geometric designs. When using a stitch larger than 1 mesh, it will nearly always be necessary to fill in corners or edges. Do as much of the stitch

14

as you can, then use Half Cross, Reverse Half Cross, a whole Cross, or whatever best complements the stitch you have been using.

You will find, as you read other sources of needlepoint instruction, that different names are sometimes used for the same stitch. As far as I am concerned, this really isn't important. As long as the stitch looks good and suits your purpose, it really doesn't matter what it's called. For our purposes, however, I have tried to designate each stitch by its most usual name.

GENERAL WORKING INSTRUCTIONS
(Making a sampler)

I have always been reluctant to spend time and effort, not to mention the cost of material, on something that will not be utilized; and I hesitate to recommend that others do this. I suggest, therefore, that you make a sampler of the stitches you are about to learn. Since you will need both mono and penelope canvas for stitches that must be used on only a particular type of canvas, a patchwork sampler pillow using mono on one side and penelope on the other would be just right. Ten to 12 squares per 1″ is best, and each piece should be at least 10″ × 10″. Prepare your canvas as described in the previous chapter, ironing it if necessary and masking the raw edges. Using any scraps of yarn you have lying about, work at least 2 sq.″ of each stitch to gain proficiency and to obtain a clear idea of the effect of the stitch within a needlepoint item. Remember to leave at least 1″ unworked on all sides. Wherever possible, mark your canvas to avoid constant counting of meshes. I have described 37 different stitches in this chapter, some of which have more than a single variation. After you have mastered all these stitches, you may want to experiment further on your sampler, using alternate color combinations, different types of yarn, beads or whatever.

·When both canvases are worked, the "patches" may be

accented and defined by embroidering an outline stitch around them in black or other contrasting yarn. For information on finishing the sampler as a pillow, see Chapter 4 and the end of the instructions for the Concentric Squares Pillow in Chapter 5.

Unless otherwise mentioned, each stitch may be worked on either mono or penelope canvas. Although up to now I have talked principally about holes or squares in the canvas, it will be easier to work the stitches in terms of meshes. A mesh is the intersection of a horizontal and a vertical thread of mono canvas. In the case of penelope canvas, it is where the double vertical and double horizontal threads intersect. I should warn you, however, that in other needlepoint sources the word mesh has the same meaning as square or hole.

In all except Loop and Fringe stitch, *the first and every odd step of a stitch involves bringing your needle up from the under side of the canvas. The second and every even step requires you to push your needle down into the canvas from the upper side.* If you work your stitches in these 2 distinct movements, using the numbers on the diagrams as a guide, you should have no problem following the instructions.

Be sure to remember, in working succeeding stitches and /or rows, to cover every single mesh of canvas. The bottom of one row will fall in the same holes as the top of the row beneath

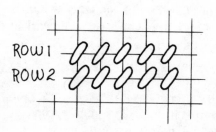

Diagram 6

it (Diagram 6). To insure optimum evenness in your work, always pull the thread through at an even tension. If your thread has become twisted, hold your canvas horizontally and allow the thread to hang down freely: the weight of the needle will cause it to turn about until the thread is untwisted.

Finally, some stitches are enhanced by an outline of back-stitches. These are done in the following manner. Bring your needle out where you want your backstitching to begin. Work from right to left horizontally, and top to bottom vertically. Push your needle in, 2 meshes away, and bring it out in the hole you just skipped. Repeat to end of row. Always bring your needle out on the same side of the thread that you did with the previous stitch (Diagram 7).

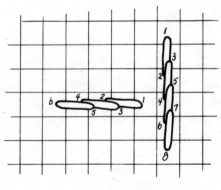

Diagram 7

STARTING AND ENDING OFF

Never start or end off with a knot; it usually unravels, and when it doesn't, it creates a bump. To start, leave at least 1″ of thread on the under side of the canvas. The larger the stitch, the longer this thread-end should be. Hold this loose end down with the middle finger of your left hand (right, if you are left-handed) and work the first 5 or 6 stitches so that the thread is covered in back of the work (Diagram 8a).

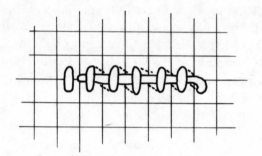

Diagram 8a

To finish off, either run your needle under several stitches on the under side of your canvas (Diagram 8b), or weave the needle in and out of the backs of several stitches (Diagram 8c). Then cut your thread.

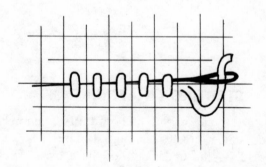

Diagram 8b

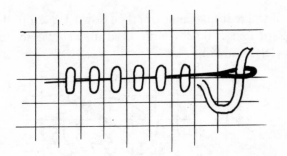

Diagram 8c

Never carry your thread loosely across the back of your work to begin another section: always weave it into the back of completed stitches or begin anew at the next section. This same rule applies to stitches whose rows can only be worked in a single direction.

TRUE NEEDLEPOINT STITCHES

While the next 2 stitches, as well as the Half Cross (in the following section), look identical from the front, each varies in durability due to the difference in the way they cover the back of the canvas.

1. Continental

This is sometimes called the Tent stitch and is the most commonly used needlepoint stitch. It covers the canvas diagonally in back as well as in front and is therefore very durable for items that will receive much wear. Work from right to left in horizontal rows. At the end of each row, turn your work upside down and work from right to left again.

Picture a square which is made up of 4 holes and which is located in the top right corner of the area to be worked. Bring your needle up in the bottom left hole of these 4, then down in the top right. Bring your needle up 1 mesh to the left of where it first came up, then down 1 mesh to the left of where it first went down. Proceed in this manner to end of row (Diagram 9a).

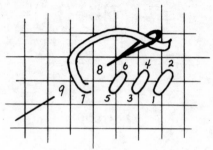

Diagram 9a

Turn your work upside down. Bring your needle up in the same hole as the top of the second stitch from the right of the row just worked. Push it in, 1 diagonal mesh to the right — i.e., 1 vertical mesh above the last stitch of the previous row. Bring it up 1 mesh to the left of where it first came up in this row, then down 1 mesh to the left of where it first went down in this row. Complete the row and turn your work upside down (Diagram 9b).

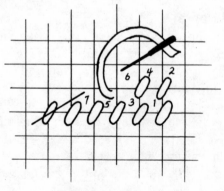

Diagram 9b

Your 2 finished rows are now at the top; the next row to be worked is below them. Bring your needle up 1 mesh beneath the last stitch in the second row, in lower left corner of stitch to be worked. Repeat your third row in the same manner described above (Diagram 9c).

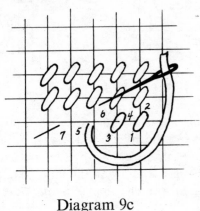

Diagram 9c

2. Basketweave

This stitch is sometimes called the Diagonal or Diagonal Tent stitch. It is even more durable than the Continental, as the thread is literally woven into the canvas. It is worked in diagonal rows, starting in the upper right corner. Begin by working 2 Continental stitches (Diagrams 10a, 10b). Bring

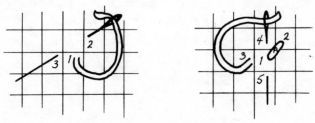

Diagrams 10a, 10b

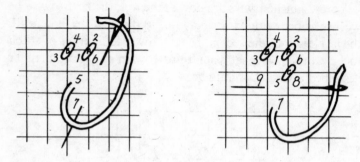

Diagrams 10c, 10d

your needle up 1 mesh below your first stitch and work 2 stitches, one below the other (4 stitches Diagrams 10a, 10b — now worked). Next, bring your needle up 1 mesh to the left of your third stitch. Following the large diagram (Diagram 10e), work the fifth stitch. Stitches 6 and 7 are to the left of stitches 1 and 2.

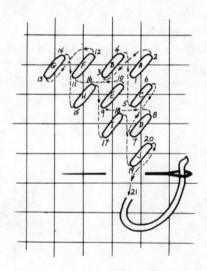

Diagram 10e

Remember that when you are working down, the needle is carried vertically across the back of your work except for the first and last stitches, when it is slanted. When working up, the needle is carried horizontally across the back of your work except for the first and last stitches, when it is slanted.

CROSS STITCH VARIATIONS

1. Half Cross

Rapidly becoming the most used needlepoint stitch, the Half Cross stitch resembles Continental and Basketweave on the front but not on the back of the canvas. Because it covers so little of the back, it is more economical than the true needlepoint stitches, but for the same reason, it is far less durable and is best suited to an item that will not require much wear — e.g., a wall hanging. The Half Cross stitch should be worked *only on penelope canvas,* as it will become distorted on mono. Work in horizontal rows from left to right, turning your work upside down to change rows.

Consider, again, a square of 4 holes in the top left corner of the section to be worked. Bring your needle up in the lower left hole. Covering 1 diagonal mesh, push your needle into the top right hole. Bring your needle up 1 mesh below where it just went in, to begin your next stitch. Proceed thus from left to right to complete row (Diagram 11a).

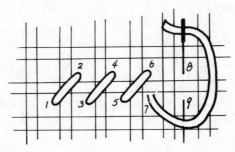

Diagram 11a

Turn your work upside down. Bring your needle up 1 mesh above where it just went in. Work a row of stitches from left to right as you did in the first row (Diagram 11b).

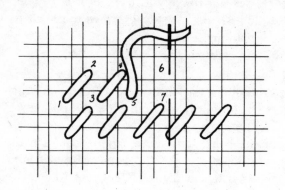

Diagram 11b

To begin the third row, turn your work upside down and bring the needle up 1 mesh below where it just went in (Diagram 11c).

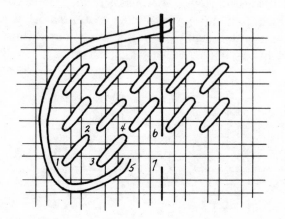

Diagram 11c

2. Cross

This stitch adds some texture to your work and is useful if your yarn does not cover the canvas adequately. It should be worked on penelope canvas.

Do a row of Half Cross stitch. Bring your needle up as if you were going to make 1 more stitch. Push it in 1 diagonal mesh to the left, crossing the stitch just worked. Bring it up one mesh below and cross the next stitch towards the left. Complete the row in this manner (Diagram 12a).

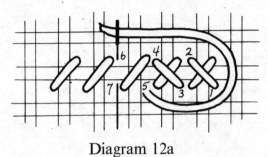

Diagram 12a

You are now back where you started. Bring your needle up 1 mesh below your first Cross stitch. Continue, doing a row of Half Cross stitch from left to right, then a row of Reverse Half Cross stitch over the first row (Diagram 12b).

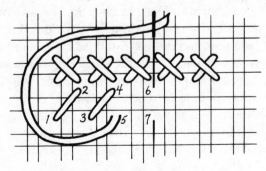

Diagram 12b

3. Knit

This is sometimes called the Lazy Knit stitch. Since it is composed of alternate rows of Half Cross and Reserve Half Cross, it should be worked only on penelope canvas.

Do a row of Half Cross stitch from left to right. Do not turn your work upside down. Bring your needle up 2 meshes below where it just went in and do a row of Reverse Half Cross stitch from right to left (Diagram 13).

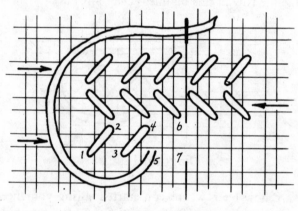

Diagram 13

4. Slanting Gobelin

This is also known as Oblique Gobelin. It does not really fall into the category of Cross Stitch Variations, but I have placed it here for two reasons. Essentially it is an elongated Half Cross stitch (and should therefore be worked only on penelope canvas) and it is a prerequisite for working the Oblong Cross stitch, to be described next.

All gobelin stitches cover 2, 3, 4 or 5 vertical meshes, depending on the effect desired. It is quickly worked and is therefore suitable for backgrounds. In this case we will be working the stitch over 1 horizontal and 2 vertical meshes of canvas.

Bring your needle up on the left side of the area to be

worked, 2 meshes below where you want the top of your first row to be. Insert it 1 mesh to the right and 2 meshes up. Bring your needle up 2 meshes below where it just went in, to begin the next stitch. Complete the row in this manner (Diagram 14a).

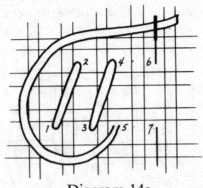

Diagram 14a

Turn your work upside down. Bring the needle up 2 meshes above where it was last inserted to begin the first stitch of the second row. Work from left to right (Diagram 14b).

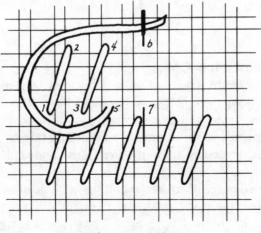

Diagram 14b

5. Oblong Cross

Work in the same manner as regular Cross stitch. On penelope canvas, do a row of Slanting Gobelin as above, covering 1 horizontal and 2 vertical meshes of canvas. Then work a row of Reverse Slanting Gobelin over this row. You need not turn your work upside down between rows, since you will always be ready to begin a new row on the left side (Diagram 15).

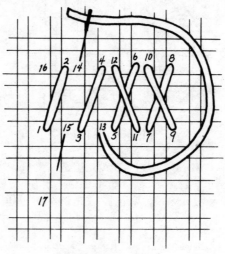

Diagram 15

6. Three Stitch Cross

This interesting textural stitch is worked in vertical rows from bottom to top. It may be worked on either mono or penelope canvas and is particularly good for covering your canvas when you are using a somewhat thin thread. It covers 2 diagonal meshes in both directions, and 2 horizontal meshes.

Bring your needle up in the bottom left hole of the area to be worked; insert it 2 meshes to the right and 2 up. Bring it out 2 meshes to the left; insert it 2 meshes to the right and 2 down. A cross has been worked. Next, bring it out in the empty hole on the left between the 2 diagonal stitches; insert it 2 meshes to the right. Bring it out in the top left hole of the stitch you have just worked and you are ready to begin your next stitch. Begin your next row by bringing the needle up in the same hole as the bottom right corner of your first stitch (Diagram 16).

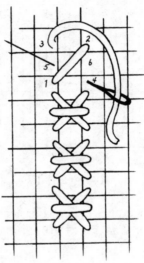

Diagram 16

7. Double Cross

This stitch, sometimes called the Smyrna Cross, looks like an 8-pointed star. In keeping with the name Double Cross, it is actually 2 superimposed crosses — 1 large upright and 1 small diagonal. The larger covers 4 meshes vertically and 4 horizontally. The smaller covers 2 diagonal meshes in each direction, in the traditional Cross stitch configuration.

Bring your needle up in a hole on the left, 2 meshes below where you want your work to begin. Insert it 4 meshes to the right. Bring it up 2 meshes to the left and 2 up. Insert it 4 meshes below. You have completed the larger cross. To begin the smaller cross, bring your needle up 1 mesh to the right and up of where it *first* came up. Insert it 2 meshes to the right and 2 down. Bring it up 2 meshes to the left. Insert it 2 meshes to the right and 2 up. Bring it up in the same hole as the right of your horizontal stitch and you are ready to begin your next stitch (Diagram 17a).

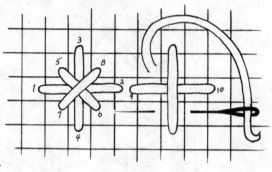

Diagram 17a

Begin your next row by bringing your needle up at the bottom of your first stitch (Diagram 17b).

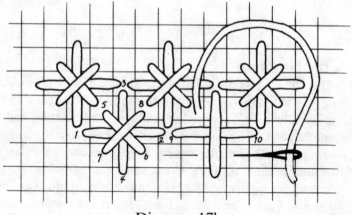

Diagram 17b

8. Large and Small Cross

This stitch and the Rice stitch, to be described next, are most effective when 2 contrasting colors are used. An even more interesting effect may be obtained if the large crosses are worked in a heavier weight yarn.

Do the large crosses first, working each cross individually. The large crosses cover 4 diagonal meshes each way. The small crosses cover 2 horizontal and 2 vertical meshes worked in the diamond-shaped space where 2 larger crosses meet. I find it easiest to do the large crosses in vertical rows, top to bottom, and the small crosses in horizontal rows, left to right. Your work may be turned upside down between rows (Diagram 18).

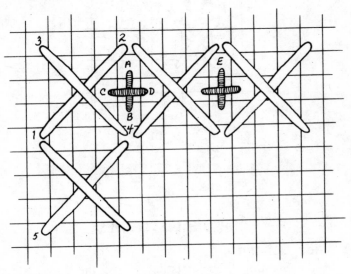

Diagram 18

9. Rice

Work the large crosses first, covering 2 diagonal meshes each way. There will be 1 empty hole between each point of the large Cross stitch. Using these holes and a contrasting thread, cross each point of the large Cross stitch covering 1 diagonal mesh. Follow the diagram for the order in which the stitches are worked (Diagram 19).

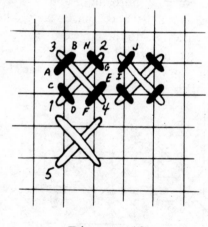

Diagram 19

DIAGONAL STITCHES

1. Wide Gobelin

In the Slanting Gobelin (stitch #4 of the Cross Stitch Variations), the stitch was higher than it was wide. The Wide Gobelin, as the name implies, is wider than it is high. In this case we will cover 3 horizontal and 2 vertical meshes. Work from left to right and turn your work upside down to change rows (Diagram 20).

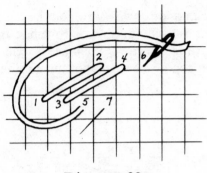

Diagram 20

2. Encroaching Gobelin

This stitch works quickly, but I'm not very fond of it, as it doesn't cover the canvas well and has a "loose" appearance.

Do a row of Slanting Gobelin, covering 1 horizontal and 5 vertical meshes of canvas (Diagram 21a).

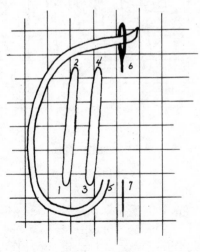

Diagram 21a

Turn your work upside down. Bring your needle up 4 meshes above where it just went in; insert it 1 mesh to the right and 5 meshes up. Complete row. Your needle will come up 1 mesh below the top of the stitches of the previous row (Diagram 21b).

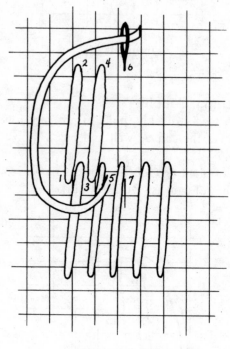

Diagram 21b

To begin your third row, turn your work upside down and bring your needle up 4 meshes below where it just went in. Your needle will now go in 1 mesh above the bottom of the stitches of the previous row (Diagram 21c).

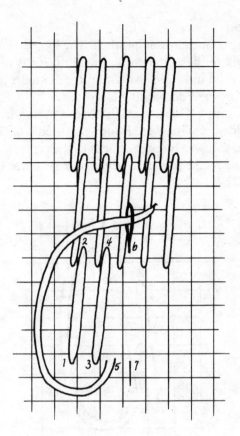

Diagram 21c

If you are using a contrasting thread for alternate rows, do not turn your work upside down between rows. Begin each row 4 meshes beneath the first stitch of the previous row. Do work your rows in order rather than working every other row in the first color and then filling in the alternate rows in your second color: you're almost sure to have miscounted somewhere along the way.

3. Knotted

This is also an encroaching stitch. The long diagonal stitch is "knotted" in the center with a small diagonal stitch going in the opposite direction. As a result, Knotted stitch is not as "loose" as the Encroaching Gobelin.

Do 1 Slanting Gobelin stitch covering 1 horizontal and 5 vertical meshes of canvas. Bring your needle up 1 mesh to the left and 2 down. Insert it 1 mesh to the right and 1 down. Bring it up 2 meshes down to begin your next Knotted stitch (Diagram 22a).

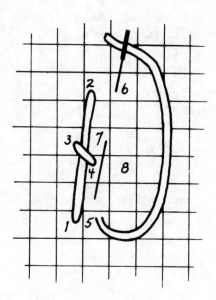

Diagram 22a

If you are working in a single color, turn your work upside down to begin the next row. If not, begin again at the left side with your second color. Since the second and subsequent rows encroach on the previous row, bring your needle up 4 vertical meshes away from the last row (Diagram 22b).

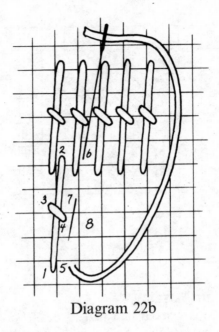

Diagram 22b

4. Florentine Mosaic

This stitch forms a pretty pattern of its own, especially if 2 or more colors are used. Work in diagonal rows, covering 1 mesh diagonally, then 2, as in Diagram 23a. For the second and subsequent rows, do a short stitch adjacent to a long, and vice versa (Diagram 23b).

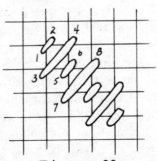

Diagram 23a

38

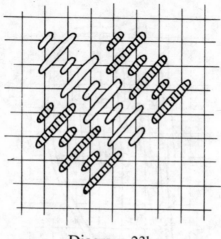

Diagram 23b

5. Hungarian Mosaic

This mosaic is worked in a pattern of a short stitch, followed by a long, followed by a second short. It is very similar to the Florentine except that it is worked in horizontal rather than diagonal rows. The overall design created is of straight, diagonal stripes — a line of short stitches, then of the long, alternating across the canvas.

You will find it easiest to do if you do not turn your work upside down between rows, but always start on the left and work towards the right. You will note from the numbering in the diagram that each stitch is worked from the top right to the bottom left corner.

The pattern begins with 1 short stitch in the upper left corner of the area to be worked. Bring your needle up at the top of the first stitch, 1 mesh away from the left edge; insert it 1 mesh down and to the left. To work the first long stitch of the design, bring the needle up 1 mesh to the right of where it first came up; insert it 1 mesh below the bottom of the short stitch. Bring it up 1 mesh to the right and 1 mesh above (i.e. across from the bottom of the initial short stitch); and push it in, 1 mesh to the left and 1 below (next to the bottom of the long stitch). Bring your needle up 1 mesh to the right of your long stitch, and you are ready to repeat the pattern (Diagram 24).

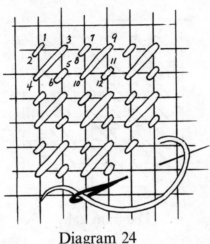

Diagram 24

You will notice that the short stitches form a straight diagonal line and the long stitches form a straight diagonal line.

6. Cashmere

Cashmere covers diagonally 1–2–2–1 mesh, as shown in Diagram 25a.

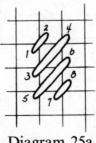

Diagram 25a

There are 2 ways of working rows. You may work in horizontal rows from left to right, in which case your work will look like Diagram 25b. Or you may work in diagonal rows to make your work look like Diagram 25c. If you do the latter, the last short stitch of the first Cashmere becomes the

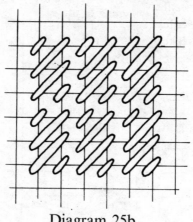

Diagram 25b

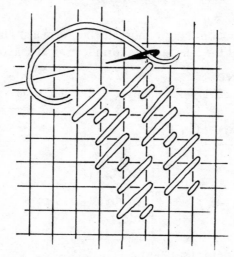

Diagram 25c

first short stitch of the second Cashmere. I personally find the former simpler to work, but it's up to you and the effect you desire.

7. Scotch

Almost every needlepoint source I've seen has a different description for Scotch stitch. In addition, sometimes the Checker and Checkerboard stitches, which I have listed separately, are described as Scotch stitch variations.

The Scotch stitch is 5 or 7 diagonal stitches getting longer, then shorter. The variations you can obtain by using different color combinations, by varying the direction of the diagonals from stitch to stitch, or by crossing the stitch are virtually endless. This is great for experimentation.

I will describe a 5-stitch Scotch, using the same direction throughout.

Bring your needle up 1 mesh down from the top at the left of the area to be worked. Working diagonally, cover 1–2–3–2–1 mesh, as in the diagram. If you wish to do the Crossed Scotch, bring your needle up in the square marked *A* and insert it at *B*. Begin your next stitch in the same hole as the top of your second 2-mesh diagonal (Diagram 26).

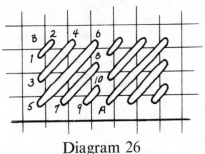

Diagram 26

8. Milanese

My nickname for this stitch is Christmas Tree stitch. Do a few square inches, and you'll see why.

Work in diagonal rows starting at the left top corner. Cover 1-2-3-4 meshes diagonally in a row as shown in Diagram 27a. Bring your needle up 3 meshes down and 2 to the left to begin the next Milanese stitch.

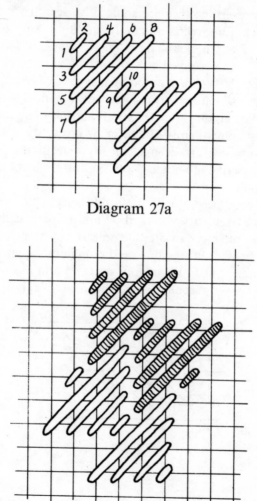

Diagram 27a

Diagram 27b

You may work your next row from top left to bottom right once again or turn your work upside down, as you prefer. Just remember that a 4-mesh stitch will be adjacent to a 1-mesh stitch, and a 3-mesh stitch will be adjacent to a 2-mesh stitch (Diagram 27b).

9. Checkerboard

This is a 9-stitch Scotch with the direction (and usually color) changing with each alternate square. The squares can later be outlined with backstitch (see beginning of this chapter) in a contrasting color, if desired. You may work the squares horizontally, vertically or diagonally, whichever you find most convenient. Personally, I usually work in diagonal rows, completing all the stitches in one direction and color at a time (Diagram 28).

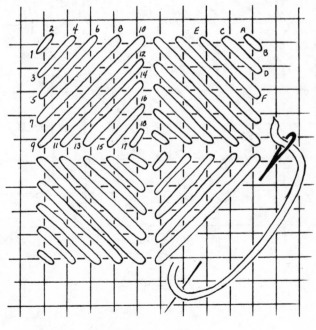

Diagram 28

10. Checker

This stitch consists of alternating squares of Scotch stitch and Half Cross or Continental. If you use a 5-stitch Scotch, the Half Cross or Continental squares will have 9 stitches. In this case, we illustrate a 7-stitch Scotch alternating with squares of 16 Half Cross or Continental stitches (Diagram 29).

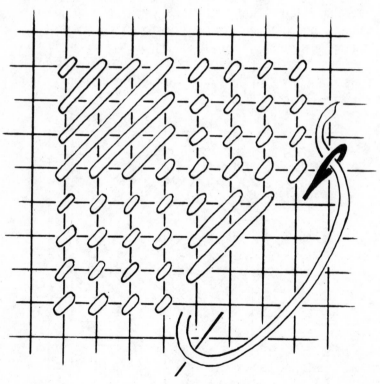

Diagram 29

11. Byzantine

This is a stepped Slanting Gobelin. Each stitch covers 1 horizontal and 3 vertical meshes. Do 4 stitches in a row horizontally; then do 3 in a row vertically, under the fourth horizontal stitch. In other words, the fourth horizontal stitch becomes your first vertical stitch, and the fourth vertical stitch becomes the first horizontal stitch of your next step. In succeeding rows, the top of each stitch will enter the same hole as the bottom of the stitch of the previous row (Diagram 30).

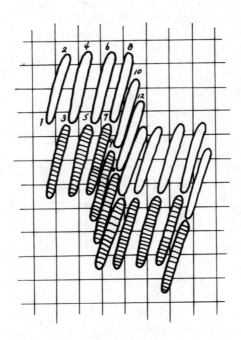

Diagram 30

12. Jacquard

This stitch, like Byzantine, is worked in steps. You may work any number of stitches in a step, but keep that number consistent for each step and each row. Remember that the last stitch of your vertical step becomes the first stitch of your horizontal step, and vice versa. The first row is worked covering 2 diagonal meshes, the next covers 1 diagonal mesh. The diagram illustrates a 5-stitch Jacquard (Diagram 31).

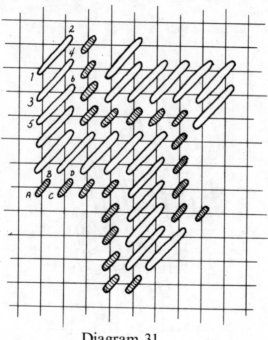

Diagram 31

TREE STITCHES

The following 4 stitches have treē-like names — with the exception of the Herringbone. Needless to say, you need not limit these stitches to working trees in a design.

1. Stem

Do not confuse the needlepoint Stem stitch with that of embroidery or crewel. If comparison with embroidery is to be made, it is more like the Satin stitch.

Start at the left or right, whichever you prefer, but work each row from top to bottom. Cover 4 diagonal meshes with each stitch and alternate the direction of the diagonals for each row (Diagram 32a).

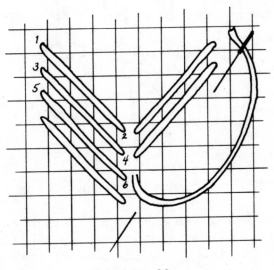

Diagram 32a

If you wish, do a row of backstitch in a contrasting color between either each row, or every other row (where the "V" is formed) (Diagram 32b).

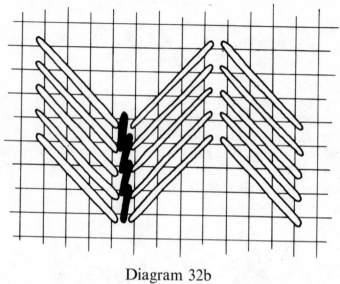

Diagram 32b

2. Fern

This stitch has a lovely texture, but it uses a great deal of yarn.

Bring your needle up in the top left hole of the area to be worked; insert it 2 meshes down and 2 to the right. Bring it up 1 mesh to the left; insert it 2 meshes to the right and up. Bring it out 1 mesh below where it first came out, to begin your next stitch. Work your rows vertically, top to bottom (Diagram 33a).

The "V" space at the top of the row may be filled with a small Cross stitch. Do a Half Cross and a Reverse Half Cross stitch on either side at the bottom of the row (Diagram 33b).

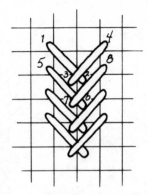

Diagram 33a

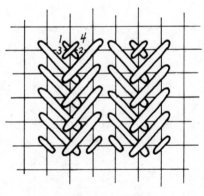

Diagram 33b

3. Herringbone

Herringbone has a lovely woven effect when worked in 1 color. It is even more interesting, however, when worked in 2 or more colors. The basic structure of the stitch is similar to Fern stitch.

Work in horizontal rows, always from left to right. Bring your needle up in the top left hole of the area to be worked; insert it 2 meshes down and 2 to the right. Bring it up 1 mesh to the left; insert it 2 meshes up and to the right. Bring it out 1 mesh to the left to begin your next stitch (Diagram 34a).

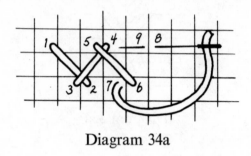

Diagram 34a

Begin your next row 1 mesh below where your needle first came up for the first stitch of the first row (Diagram 34b).

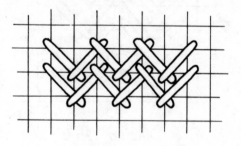

Diagram 34b

4. Leaf

This is a fairly complicated stitch to explain, but not that difficult to master if you follow the diagram. It is one of the prettiest needlepoint stitches, so do take the trouble to learn it. It is fairly difficult to fit this stitch into a rectangular shape. It is advisable to work it in the center of a piece and fit other stitches such as Half Cross or Continental around it.

Work from right to left. Bring your needle up 3 meshes from the right and 9 meshes below the top right corner of the area to be worked. This is the bottom center of your first Leaf. Insert your needle 3 meshes to the right and 4 up. Do 2 more stitches exactly like the first, working upwards so that the beginning and end of each is 1 mesh above the corresponding part of the previous stitch. Bring your needle up 1 mesh above where it last came up; insert it 2 meshes to the right and 4 up. Bring it up 1 mesh above where it last came up; insert it 1 mesh to the right and 4 up. Bring it up 2 meshes above where it last came up; and do an upright stitch covering 3 meshes. Complete the other side to match (Diagram 35a).

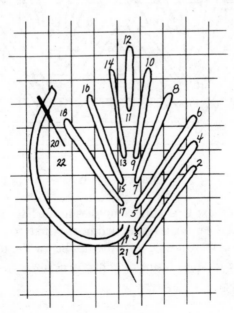

Diagram 35a

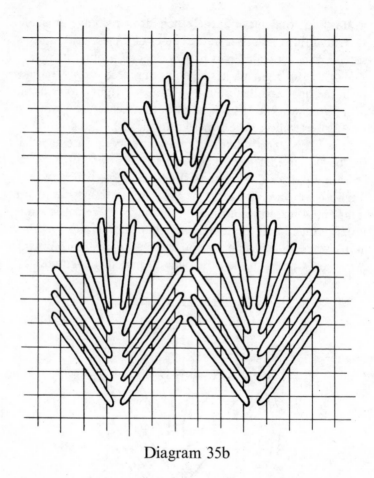

Diagram 35b

Begin your next Leaf stitch 6 meshes to the left of the base of your first Leaf. After completing the first row of Leaf stitches, bring your needle up 9 meshes below the top of the first stitch of the first Leaf in the previous row.

UPRIGHT STITCHES

Upright stitches are best worked on mono canvas as they tend not to cover penelope adequately.

1. Upright Gobelin

Like all gobelins, this stitch may cover 2, 3, 4, or 5 vertical meshes of canvas. I will describe a simple 2 mesh Gobelin. Work from left to right and turn your work upside down to change rows.

Bring your needle up on the left side, 2 meshes below the top of the area to be worked; push it in 2 meshes above. Bring it out 1 mesh to the right of where it first came out and you are ready to begin your next stitch (Diagram 36a).

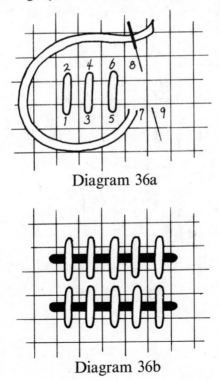

Diagram 36a

Diagram 36b

Upright Gobelin can be very effective if worked over tramé (see Chapter 2) of a different color yarn. This can only be done if you work a 2 mesh Gobelin. Tramé horizontally the mesh you will be skipping, i.e., every second horizontal row (Diagram 36b).

2. Brick

This is slightly more interesting than Upright Gobelin. Begin by bringing your needle out on the left, 3 meshes below the top of the area to be worked. Do 1 Upright Gobelin stitch, covering 2 meshes of canvas. Bring your needle up 1 mesh to the right and 1 down of where it just went in. Insert it 2 meshes above. Bring it out 3 meshes down and 1 to the right of where it just went in and you are ready to begin your next stitch. Turn your work upside down to change rows (Diagram 37).

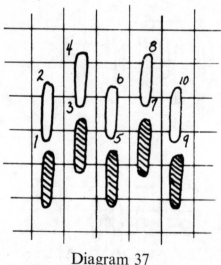

Diagram 37

3. Parisian

This is often confused with Hungarian stitch, to be described next. They are easy to differentiate if you remember

55

that in Parisian embroidery a short stitch falls directly below a long, whereas in Hungarian embroidery all short stitches are beneath each other and all long stitches are beneath each other.

Cover alternately 1 vertical mesh, then 3, working from left to right. The longer stitch should extend 1 mesh above and 1 below the shorter. If you are working in 1 color, turn your work upside down to begin the next row. If not, begin at the left again with your second color. Do a short stitch if you are above or below a long, and vice versa (Diagram 38).

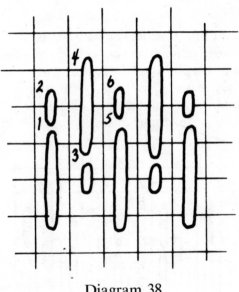

Diagram 38

4. Hungarian

Working from left to right, do 3 upright stitches covering 2–4–2 vertical meshes. Skip 1 horizontal mesh and repeat to end of row (Diagram 39a).

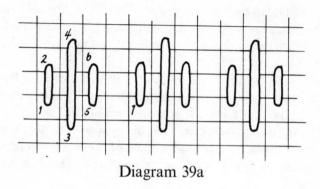

Diagram 39a

On the next row, whether you have turned your work up-side down or not, the mesh you will skip will be where the long stitch of the previous row has been worked. The same applies on all succeeding rows (Diagram 39b).

You will notice that all the short stitches are beneath each other, and all the long stitches are beneath each other.

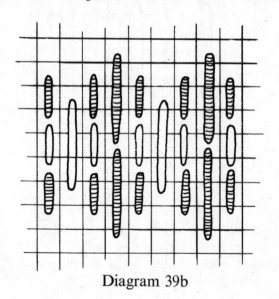

Diagram 39b

5. Old Florentine

This stitch is comprised of 2 short stitches, followed by 2 long stitches. The configuration is vertically and horizontally symmetrical. The longer stitches extend equally above and below the longer; and, on succeeding rows, the short stitches fall above or below the long ones and vice versa. Cover 1–1–3–3 meshes, 2–2–6–6 or 3–3–9–9, for example. I illustrate the last, since it is, as I understand, the customary number of meshes over which Old Florentine is worked (Diagram 40).

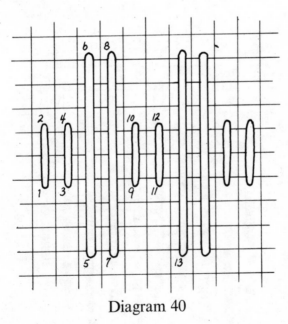

Diagram 40

6. Bargello

Bargello has recently become one of the most popular of needlepoint stitches. It is also known as Flame or Florentine, but basically it is an Upright Gobelin done in steps. Some needlepoint sources are very specific about this stitch: cover 3 meshes and begin the next stitch 1 mesh above or below the last, or cover 4 meshes and begin the next stitch 2 meshes above or below the last. I feel that the possibilities of this stitch are virtually endless and it is silly to limit yourself in this way. So I say do the stitch as long or as short as you wish, do the next stitch as many meshes above or below the former as you wish, have each row composed of the same size stitch

Flame design

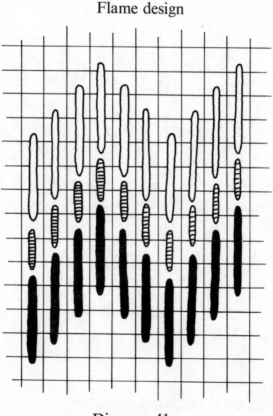

Diagram 41a

or vary the stitch length from row to row, as you wish. If you think it might work, try it — it probably will (Diagrams 41a, 41b, 41c).

Abstract design

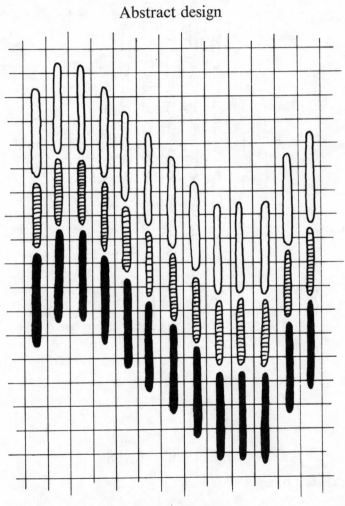

Diagram 41b

Geometric design

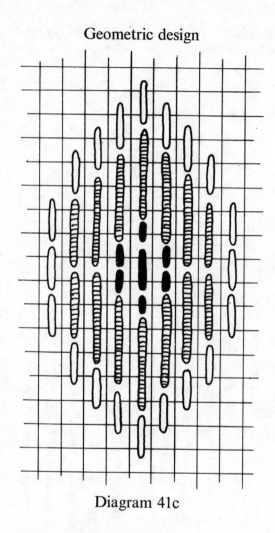

Diagram 41c

NOVELTY STITCHES

These stitches don't fit into any of the above categories. They are useful to know, however, so I am including them here.

1. Diamond Eyelet

This stitch is worked from the center hole of the stitch, out. You may work your rows from left to right or right to left, or starting at the top or bottom, whichever you find easiest.

Begin by bringing your needle up 4 meshes away from any edge of the area to be worked. Insert it 4 vertical meshes upward. Bring your needle up at the center hole (the same hole where it first came up) and insert it 3 meshes up and 1 to the right. Bring it up at center; insert it 1 mesh up and 3 to the right. Bring it up at center and do a horizontal stitch to the right covering 4 meshes. Complete the other 3 sides of the diamond to match, using Diagram 42a as a guide.

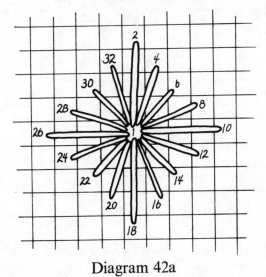

Diagram 42a

Begin your next stitch 4 horizontal meshes away from the end of any horizontal stitch. On succeeding rows, the sides of the diamond will enter the same holes as the sides of the adjacent diamonds (Diagram 42b).

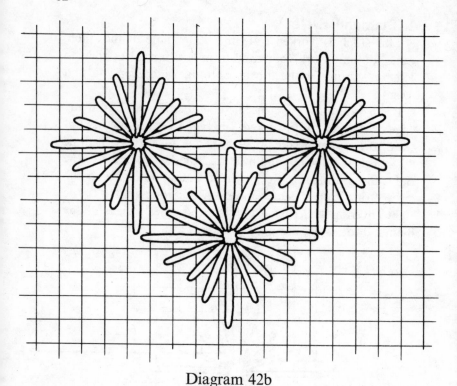

Diagram 42b

If you wish, you may outline each Diamond Eyelet with backstitching of a contrasting color.

2. Star

In this stitch, as in the Diamond Eyelet, the stitches radiate from the center hole. This time, though, there are only 8 radiations, not 16, and your stitch forms a square shape, not a diamond. Most needlepoint sources instruct you to bring your needle up at the sides and push it in at the center, but you may work it in the same manner as Diamond Eyelet, i.e., up at the center hole, if you prefer. The diagram illustrates the former method, since that is the "correct" way of doing the Star. Work your rows the way you choose, covering 2 meshes with each radiation. Work backstitch around the completed stars if you like (Diagram 43).

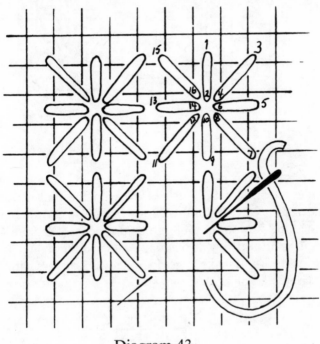

Diagram 43

3. Chain

This is actually an embroidery stitch worked on canvas, where it gives a knitted effect. Work in vertical rows, top to bottom. Bring your needle up in the top left hole of the area to be worked. Insert it *in the same hole* but do not pull thread all the way through: leave a loop above the canvas. Bring needle up 1 mesh below, passing it through the loop on the way up. Make sure your thread passes *under* the needle as you bring the needle up, as in Diagram 44a.

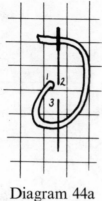 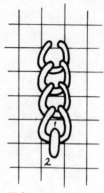

Diagram 44a   Diagram 44b

Continue your row, inserting your needle in the same hole and bringing it out 1 mesh below with the thread passing under the needle. To finish off a row, simply insert your needle 1 mesh below your last loop to hold it down (Diagram 44b). Begin your next row at the top, 1 mesh to the right.

If you wish to make larger loops, cover 2 meshes with each stitch instead of 1 (Diagram 44c).

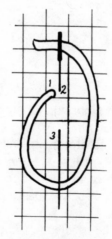

Diagram 44c

4. Loop and Fringe

The Loop stitch has loops, as the name implies. If you cut these loops, you have the Fringe stitch. This is a difficult stitch to master, but it's gorgeous, especially for rugs, so do learn it.

This is the only stitch that you begin with your needle and yarn *in front* of the canvas. All odd numbers on the diagrams, therefore, refer to inserting your needle into the canvas front to back: even numbers refer to bringing your needle up from the back of the canvas to the front.

This stitch should be done on penelope canvas. You may use mono if you work over 2 meshes of canvas instead of 1.

Work in horizontal rows, always from left to right, and begin at the bottom of the area to be covered. If you want full loops or fringe, do your rows every mesh. For a sparser effect skip 1 or 2 meshes between rows.

With needle and yarn in front of work, insert needle into canvas and bring it up 1 mesh below, leaving about 1″ at the end of your thread when pulling it through. With your left thumb (right, if you are left-handed) hold this end down below your working row. Insert your needle in the same hole as you first did and bring it out 1 mesh to the left, making sure your thread passes *under* the needle as you bring it out. Pull this stitch firmly (Diagram 45a).

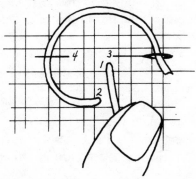

Diagram 45a

Insert your needle in the first hole once again and bring it out 1 mesh below. Leave a loop of the desired length before pulling your thread all the way through. Wrap this loop around your non-working thumb, a pencil, ruler, or piece of firm cardboard. This is your gauge and will ensure that all your loops are of uniform size. Hold this loop down until you have completed the stitch (Diagram 45b).

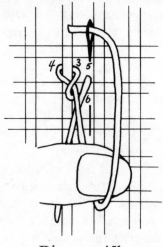

Diagram 45b

Insert your needle 1 mesh to the right of where it just went in and bring it out 1 mesh to the left, i.e., where it first went in. Make sure your thread passes under the needle on the left (Diagram 45c).

Begin your next stitch by inserting your needle where it last went in and bringing it out 1 mesh below, leaving a loop around your gauge. Insert it 1 mesh to the right of where it just went in and bring it out 1 mesh to the left, making sure the thread passes under your needle (Diagram 45d).

Begin your next row 1 or more meshes above the first in the same manner as the first, with yarn and needle in front of canvas.

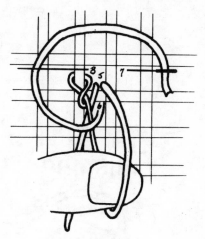

Diagram 45c

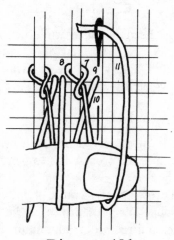

Diagram 45d

If you desire Fringe, cut the loops in half and trim if desired.

A word of caution: this stitch is *terrible* to remove, as each loop is actually knotted. So think before you stitch.

CHAPTER 4
Finishing

CLEANING

If your item has become soiled while being worked, put some carbon tetrachloride or other dry-cleaning fluid on a cloth or sponge and lightly wipe your work. Needlepoint items should always be dry-cleaned.

BLOCKING

The most grossly misshapen article can be blocked back into shape. Sometimes the process has to be repeated several times, but it can be done.

You need plain brown paper, a piece of flat wood (plywood is good) large enough for your project to lie flat on, transparent tape, a pen, and rustproof (aluminum is best) thumb tacks or push pins.

Draw the dimensions of your original pattern, including the edges not worked, on a piece of brown paper. Say you have made a 14″ square pillow and left a 1″ border all around. You will draw a 16″ square on the brown paper. This first step may be done when you make your original pattern (see Chapter 2). Mark the center of each side. Tape the brown paper to the board, using transparent tape.

If your item is badly misshapen, wet it thoroughly, then roll in a turkish towel to remove excess moisture. If it is only slightly out of shape, simply dampen the back of the canvas with a wet sponge or cloth.

Lay the item right side down on the brown paper pattern. When stretching the canvas to fit the pattern, pull on opposite sides at the same time — don't just tug at a single corner. Pushing your tacks or pins into the unworked edge of the canvas rather than through the worked part, pin down the corners, then the center of each side. Placing your pins or tacks about 1″ apart, pin down the entire edge. Leave your work pinned down on the board until it is completely dry — usually 24 to 48 hours. Unpin. If your piece is still out of shape repeat the entire process as many times as necessary.

If you have made a garment or other non-rectangular item, block in the same manner. If, for example, you have made a vest, place your initial pins or tacks at the shoulders, neck, underarm, lower end of the side seam, and bottom center. Then place pins or tacks 1″ apart in between.

Your piece may have lost some of its original sizing or stiffness in the working or blocking. In many cases this does not matter, but in items such as handbags or rugs where stiffness is important, you can re-size the canvas. While it is still pinned down for blocking (it should, however, be dry) spread a *thin* layer of white glue on the back of your canvas.

MITERING CORNERS

Whenever your project has to lie flat it will be necessary to miter the corners to eliminate excessive bulk. Cut each corner diagonally, $\frac{1}{4}$″ to $\frac{1}{2}$″ away from the completed needlepoint

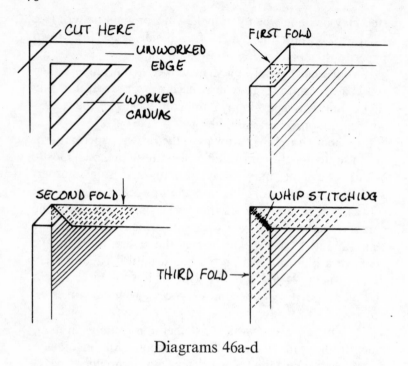

Diagrams 46a-d

(see Diagram 46a). Lay the canvas on your working surface, wrong side up. Fold the unworked canvas edge towards the wrong side in this order: 1) corner diagonal, 2) top edge, 3) side edge. You will find that the top and side edges meet in a diagonal going from the corner towards the center of the piece. Whipstitch the 2 sides of the canvas together along this diagonal, using cotton sewing thread. Repeat for other corners (Diagrams 46b, 46c, 46d).

MOUNTING PICTURES

For a small picture, 12″ × 12″ or less, cut a piece of thick cardboard the dimensions of the worked area of the canvas. For anything larger than 12″ × 12″, use thin plywood.

Stretch the canvas, right side up, over the board and pin into the edges of the board, using straight pins on cardboard and carpet tacks on plywood. Before pushing your pins or hammering your tacks all the way in, make sure your rows are straight.

Now turn the needlepoint-covered board wrong side up. Miter the corners as above. Using a strong thread such as nylon, link the top and bottom edges of canvas, then the 2 sides (Diagrams 47a, 47b,).

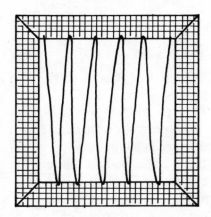 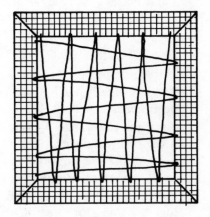

Diagrams 47a, 47b

MOUNTING SEAT COVERS

Mount the needlepoint over the original cushion. Using upholstery tacks, secure the canvas to the board on the under side of the cushion, placing tacks $1\frac{1}{2}''$ to $2''$ apart. Once again, before hammering the tacks all the way in, make certain your rows of needlepoint are straight.

You do not have to link the opposite edges of canvas on the under side of the cushion as you did when mounting a picture: the chair frame will prevent too much stress from being placed on the tacked-down parts of canvas.

GLUING

Trivets, place mats and sometimes belts can be glued to a cork or felt backing. Miter the corners of the needlepoint as above. Put a tiny dab of white glue every 2″ or 3″ on the underside of the turned down edges to keep them flat against the needlepoint. Cut the cork or felt to the exact size of the completed needlepoint piece. Spread a *light* film of white glue on the cork or felt and place the wrong side of your needlepoint on the glued side of the cork or felt. Align it perfectly and leave to dry.

SEWING

Regard your needlepoint as if it were any piece of fabric. The unworked edge is your seam allowance and should now be trimmed to about ½″ away from the last row or stitch. Keep the edges from fraying by spreading white glue along them, or by doing a machine zig-zag stitch along them.

You will be sewing your needlepoint either to another piece of needlepoint or to another type of fabric such as burlap, velvet, satin or suede. Lay the 2 pieces to be joined right sides together and machine stitch along the last row of needlepoint. It is always better to sew along worked canvas rather than unworked, as it will hold better. Sew 3 sides together, trim the corners, then turn inside out. If it is to be a stuffed item such as a pillow or pincushion, stuff at this point. Now slip stitch the last side by hand.

The above applies mainly to straight edges. If you are making a round pillow, sew ⅔ to ¾ of the circumference. Clip both layers of seam allowance every 1″ or so. Turn inside out, stuff, then slip stitch the rest of the circumference.

What about a garment that has to be lined? Say you have needlepointed the left and right fronts of a vest. The back is to be suede and it is to be lined with satin.

You have the 2 fronts. Cut 2 satin fronts for the lining.

Using your commercial pattern cut a back out of suede and another out of satin. Sew darts, if any, in needlepoint and satin fronts. Join the needlepoint front to the suede back at the side seams. Join the 3 pieces of satin together at the side seams.

Right sides together, lay your lining on the needlepoint and suede. Sew the outer garment to the lining at the arm-holes, neck and all around the sides except for about 3″ at center back. Leave shoulder seams open. Your seam line should be along the last row or stitch of needlepoint, not in the unworked canvas.

Fold the vest at the side seams so that the needlepoint fronts and suede back face each other and the lining is on the outside. At the shoulder seams, sew the needlepoint fronts to the suede back. Do not join the lining at the shoulders.

Put your hand into the opening you left (at center back) and turn the entire garment inside out. Slip stitch the front and back lining together at the shoulder seams. Slip stitch the opening at center back, and there you have it — a unique garment, all your own work.

CHAPTER 5
Projects

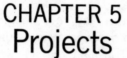

REPEAT-DESIGN BELT

Chart, Key and Notations

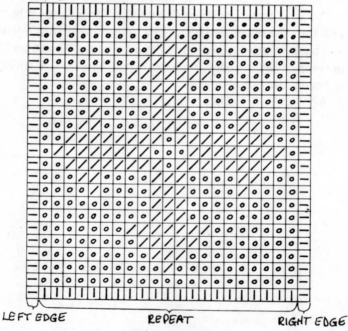

LEFT EDGE   REPEAT   RIGHT EDGE

Diagram 48

| o | Color A, Continental

| / | Color B, Continental

| I | Color C, Upright Gobelin covering 3 meshes

| — | Color D, Horizontal Gobelin covering 3 meshes

Note: Each square represents 1 stitch, not 1 mesh of canvas.

Materials

Canvas: Mono, 12-mesh gauge; width 3″; length 2″ plus waist or hip measurement. If economy is a factor, purchase only ½ yard of canvas and cut into 3″ strips. Join the canvas once or twice, depending on the length desired, as described in Chapter 2.

Yarn: Persian — 2 oz. color A, 1 oz. color B. (1 oz. yarn is equivalent to approximately 1500″–1600″ in length.

Backing Material: Vinyl, Leatherette, suede or other suitable backing material, cut to the same dimensions as the canvas.

Buckle: A 2-piece interlocking buckle. Don't use the prong type that requires holes to be punched in the belt. The one I like looks like this (Diagram 49).

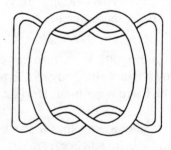

Diagram 49

Needles and Scissors: Embroidery scissors and 1 or 2 medium size tapestry needles.

Equipment

Masking tape, ruler, waterproof felt tip pen, brown paper, rust-proof thumb tacks or push pins, plywood or other soft wood large enough to accommodate the belt for blocking.

Preparation

Iron canvas with a dry iron if necessary. Cut the canvas to the above dimensions, selvedge running horizontally. Cover the raw edges with masking tape.

With waterproof felt tip pen, make 2 horizontal lines on the belt, 27 meshes apart. The distance between these 2 lines (approximately $2\frac{1}{4}''$) is the width of your belt. When measuring the length, subtract the length of your buckle from your actual waist or hip measurement. The length of the belt has to be a multiple of 20 meshes (approximately $1\frac{1}{2}''$), plus 6 meshes (about $\frac{1}{2}''$) for the two Gobelin borders. If possible, allow $\frac{1}{4}''$ to $\frac{1}{2}''$ extra, as your work will "tighten up" the canvas. If necessary for correct measurements, eliminate side borders, or have them cover more than 3 meshes. I found that 20 repeats of the basic design plus the 2 side borders gives a 33″ belt.

It is not necessary to mark your canvas further. Work from the chart for the first repeat design, then use your work and/or the chart for further reference.

Instructions

Work the belt from right to left, turning your work upside down between rows. The main body of the belt is worked in Continental stitch. There is a 3-mesh Upright Gobelin border all around.

Turn your work sideways so that a short edge is on top. Do a row Upright Gobelin stitches from left to right between the 2 horizontal pen marks. Cover 3 vertical meshes with each stitch. This is your right side border.

Turn your work so that the worked edge is on the right. Now, working from right to left, follow the portion of the chart marked "repeat." You will find it easier if you work color B first, then fill in the background and small crosses with color A. Repeat the number of times required, then do left side border.

Blocking

Follow the general instructions for blocking described in Chapter 4. The dimensions of your belt are $2\frac{1}{4}''$ wide, by the desired length. You will probably have to block several times, as this design distorts the canvas quite a bit in the working.

Finishing

Remove masking tape from the 2 long sides of the belt. Trim, $\frac{1}{2}''$ away from the Gobelin border. Do a row of machine zig-zag stitches along these edges to prevent fraying. If you do not own a sewing a machine, over-sew by hand or run a thin line of white glue along the edges.

Place your needlepoint on the backing fabric right sides together. Pin or baste, then sew 1 lengthwise seam, starting and finishing 2″ to 3″ away from the sides of the belt. Make sure that your seam line falls on the Gobelin border and not on the unworked canvas.

Now fold back along the seam just sewn, so that the wrong sides of the needlepoint and backing fabric are together. Along the other long edge turn in the seam allowance on both canvas and backing. Pin or baste in place and sew together *by hand*, using slip stitch or whipping. Once again, leave 2″ to 3″ free on each end of the seam.

Attach each part of the buckle separately. Fold back the unattached backing to keep it out of the way. Thread the canvas over the bar of the buckle toward the wrong side. Your Gobelin border should lie directly over the buckle bar. Pin or baste the side seam allowance to the wrong side of the needlepoint without removing the masking tape. Whip or slip-stitch in place (Diagram 50).

Sew the remaining portion of the lengthwise seams together.

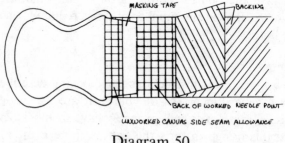

Diagram 50

Trim the side seam allowance of your backing to $\frac{1}{2}''$. Turn under and stitch by hand to the Gobelin side border.

Attach the second part of the buckle in the same manner.

CONCENTRIC SQUARE PILLOWS

Diagram

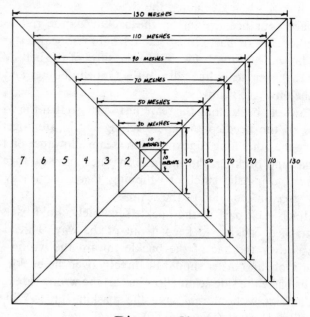

Diagram 51

Materials

Canvas: Penelope, 10-mesh gauge; 15″ × 15″.

Yarn: D.M.C. Tapestry yarn, 8-meter skeins — 5 skeins color A, 7 skeins color B, 4 skeins color C and 6 skeins color D. Use blues and greens, reds and oranges, or whatever best suits your color scheme. I used red, 2 shades of orange, and gold.

Backing Material: A 15″ × 15″ of burlap, felt, corduroy, velvet, or other suitable backing material to match or contrast with yarn colors.

Stuffing: Shredded foam rubber, torn panty-hose, a 13″ square pillow form, or any other available stuffing.

Needles and Scissors: Embroidery scissors, and 1 to 4 medium size tapestry needles.

Equipment

Masking tape, ruler, waterproof felt tip pen, brown paper, rust-proof thumb tacks or push pins, plywood or other soft wood at least 15″ × 15″ for blocking.

Preparation

Iron canvas with a dry iron if necessary. Cut to above dimensions and place masking tape along the raw edges to prevent fraying.

Following the diagram, draw 7 concentric squares on the canvas with a waterproof felt tip pen. Begin at the center and work out. Your center square (square #1) is 10 meshes square. Each consecutive square is 10 meshes away from the previous one, on all sides. Be sure to mark your canvas exactly along the grain.

Now carefully draw your diagonals. They should bisect the corners of each square. With the selvedge running vertically, mark the top of your canvas. Write "TOP" or use a symbol, whichever you prefer. Number the squares 1 to 7 from the center out, as in the diagram.

Instructions

General

1. Work your rows in order. Do not try to work all the rows of 1 color and then fill in the spaces with another.
2. Some of the stitches used do not fit naturally into a rectangular area. You will have to shorten the individual stitches along the edges so that they cover only as many meshes as needed to fit into the outline you have drawn.
3. Do not carry your thread loosely over the back of your work. Weave it into the backs of completed stitches to begin a new section.

Square #1: Do 4 Checkerboard stitches using color A in top left and bottom right corners, and color D in top right and bottom left corners. To work each complete stitch, cover mesh in a pattern of: 1–2–3–4–5–4–3–2–and 1 (Diagram 52).

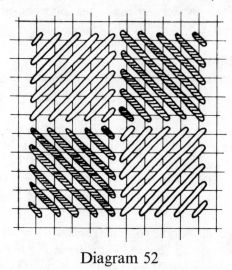

Diagram 52

Square #2: Work in Milanese stitch, alternating colors A and B for each row. Begin with B at upper left corner of square.

Cover mesh in a pattern of: 1–2–3–and 4. Work towards Square #1 (5 Milanese stitches). Now, with color A, bring needle up 1 mesh below your first B stitch, on the line you have drawn. In order to keep the square shape, you will have to cover 2–2–2–and 1 mesh for your first A stitch. Work the rest of the row covering 4–3–2–and 1 mesh, towards the center. Your last stitch will cover only 3 then 1 mesh, in order to keep the square shape.

Continue thus, working colors in alternate rows of B and A from top left to bottom right. B rows will "point" upwards, A downwards. Your first 3 rows will look like this (Diagram 53).

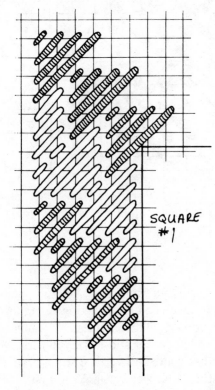

Diagram 53

Square #3: Turn your work so that the side you have marked "top" is on the left. With color D along what is now your upper left diagonal, work rows of Florentine Mosaic, alternating colors D and C for each row. Follow the general instructions. Your first 3 rows will look like this (Diagram 54).

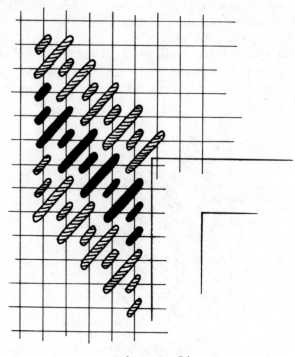

Diagram 54

Square #4: Turn your work right side up again. Work a 6-stitch Jacquard, with color A covering 2 diagonal meshes and color D covering 1 diagonal mesh of canvas. Begin with color A in top left corner and work your first step vertically. Remember that your sixth vertical stitch becomes your first horizontal stitch, and vice versa. Your first 5 rows will look like this (Diagram 55).

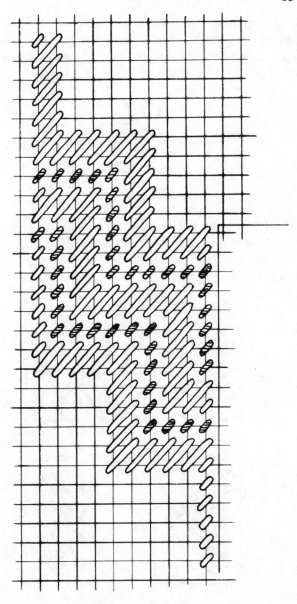

Diagram 55

Square #5: Start in top left corner with color B. Work vertical rows of Fern stitch using B and C. Begin each row with a Cross stitch and end each row with 2 small diagonal stitches on either side (Diagram 56a).

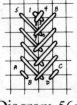

Diagram 56a

Do the Reverse Half Cross stitch in fourth row and the Half Cross stitch in fourth-to-last row along the edges of Square #4. Follow the diagrams for modification of the Fern stitch at the 4 corners of Square #4 (Diagrams 56b, 56c, 56d, 56e).

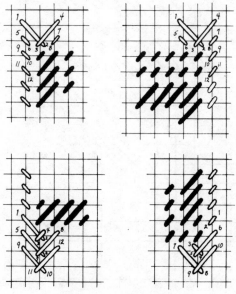

Diagrams 56b-e

Square #6: Work in the Herringbone stitch horizontally, doing alternate rows of colors D and B, beginning with D. Your first and last rows, and those along the top and bottom edges of Square #5 will seem thicker than the other rows. End each row with a short diagonal stitch (Diagrams 57a, 57b).

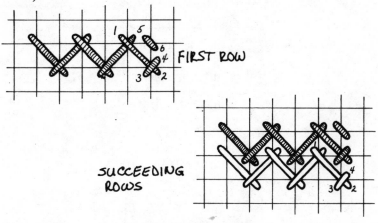

Diagrams 57a, 57b

Square #7: Do this square in the Half Cross stitch with a Cross stitch in each corner. Work each row on all 4 sides of the square, turning your work 90° at each corner so that the side you are working is on top. Work from the outside of the square towards Square #6, using colors A, B, A, C, A, D, A, C, A and B respectively. Begin by bringing your needle up on the diagonal line (Diagram 58a).

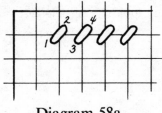

Diagram 58a

Work across row to corner, which is done like this (Diagram 58b).

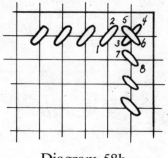

Diagram 58b

Complete other 3 sides in the same manner, working your last corner as shown (Diagram 58c).

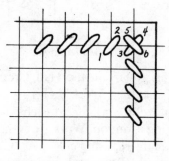

Diagram 58c

Each corner should look like this (Diagram 58d).

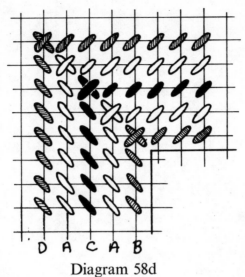

Diagram 58d

Blocking

Follow the general instructions for blocking described in Chapter 4. The worked part of the pillow should be 13″ × 13″.

Finishing

Trim the edges so that you have a $\frac{1}{2}$″ seam allowance on all 4 sides. Cut your backing fabric to the same size. Place the needlepoint and backing fabric right sides together. Sew all 4 seams, leaving about 6″ open in the center of one side. Your seam line should fall on the last row of needlepoint. Turn inside out. Stuff. Whip or slip stitch the remaining half-side by hand.